Studies in

Philemon

I0164567

Michael Penny

ISBN: 978-1-78364-522-0

www.obt.org.uk

Studies in Philemon 1

****

The Open Bible Trust
Fordland Mount, Upper Basildon,
Reading, RG8 8LU, UK.

Studies in Philemon 2

Studies in Philemon

Historically; Theologically; Practically

Contents

Page

Studies in Philemon 4

Philemon:
Historically

Philemon: Historically

The letter to Philemon, centres on three people; the Apostle Paul, the affluent Philemon, and the slave Onesimus.

Paul

Following his third missionary journey, Paul returned to Jerusalem. There he reported to James and the elders "what God had done among the Gentiles through his ministry" (Acts 21:19). However, a week later, when in the temple, Paul was the centre of a great controversy.

Some Jews from the province of Asia saw Paul at the temple. They stirred up the whole crowd and seized him, shouting, "Men of Israel, help us! This is the man who teaches all men everywhere against our people and our law and this place. And besides, he has brought Greeks into the temple area and defiled this holy place." (They had previously seen Trophimus the Ephesian in the city with Paul and assumed that Paul had brought him into the temple area.) The whole city was aroused, and the people came running from all directions. Seizing Paul, they dragged him from the temple, and immediately the gates where shut. (Acts 21:27-30).

Their accusations were false (Acts 20:21-26), but the effect was staggering. They beat Paul and were intent on killing him. It required the intervention of the Roman commander and his troops to save his life (Acts 21:31-32). Order was restored and Paul was allowed to address the crowd. However, his words had little effect. They soon shouted, "Rid the earth of him! He's not fit to live!" (Acts 22:23).

This time the commander ordered Paul to be taken into the barracks. The next day he released him and Paul was to address the Sanhedrin, the Jewish ruling council. However, his words split the council and the dispute became so violent that the commander was afraid that Paul would be torn to pieces. He ordered his troops to take Paul away from the Sanhedrin and bring him to the barracks for safety (Acts 23:9-10).

However, he was not safe there. The Jews conspired to kill Paul, but his nephew found out about it and told Paul and the commander. Then he [the commander] called two of his centurions and ordered, "Get ready a detachment of two hundred soldiers, seventy horsemen and two hundred spearmen to go to Caesarea at nine tonight. Provide mounts for Paul so that he may be taken safely to Governor Felix." (Acts 23:23-24)

However, if Paul thought he would have a fair hearing from Felix, he was wrong. Five days later the high priest Ananias and the elders and a lawyer arrived. On hearing both sides Felix postponed his decision, ostensibly until the commander arrived. However, several days later Paul was still under guard, when Felix spoke to him again. That audience ended with Felix saying, "When I find it convenient, I will send for you."However, he was hoping for a bribe from Paul, so he sent for him frequently. However, Paul did not offer any bribe and was left in prison for two years, because Felix wanted to grant a favour to the Jews (Acts 24:22-27).

Felix was succeeded by Festus, and within his first week, he went up from Caesarea to Jerusalem. There the chief priests and Jewish leaders appeared before him and presented charges against Paul. They also requested that Paul be transferred to Jerusalem, but the motive behind this was that they would ambush Paul and kill him along the way (Acts 25:1-3). However, Festus told them to present their charges against Paul at Caesarea, to where he was returning. This they did.

When Paul appeared before them, the Jews who had come down from Jerusalem brought many serious charges against him, but they could not prove any of them (Acts 25:7). However, Festus, wishing to do the Jews a favour, asked Paul if he was willing to go up to Jerusalem and stand trial there. Paul knew this was certain death and so he appealed to Caesar (Acts 25: 7-11). As a Roman citizen Paul had the right to have his case tried in

Rome, and he knew that he would have a fairer trial in Rome than he would get in Jerusalem.

For some time Paul remained in Caesarea, until it was finally decided that he should set sail for Italy (Acts 27:1). How much time had elapsed from that trouble in Jerusalem to the time he set sail for Rome, we cannot be sure, but it was well in excess of two years (Acts 24:27). However, Paul's problems were not over. *En route* to Rome they were shipwrecked on the island of Malta (Acts 27-28:1). They were there three months before leaving for Rome, where Paul was put under house arrest (Acts 28:11-16). But Paul was not soon to be free. He was there for two whole years before his case was heard (Acts 28:30).

During that time he wrote four letters (Ephesians, Colossians, Philemon and Philippians), and from those letters we find we had many visitors. Some we know well – people like Luke, Mark and Timothy – others we may be less familiar with – people like Tychicus, Aristarchus, Jesus Justus, Epaphras, Demas and Epaphroditus – and one is very crucial to our study, a runaway slave called Onesimus.

Onesimus and Philemon

Onesimus was the slave of Philemon, a man whom Paul called a "dear friend and fellow worker" (Philemon 1). Paul wrote to Philemon and said "you owe me your very self" (Philemon 19). In other words, it was through Paul's ministry that Philemon had become a believer in the Lord Jesus Christ and so had received forgiveness and the promise of eternal life.

However, we should not have the impression that Paul felt that Philemon did, actually, owe him something for coming to the Lord through Paul's teaching. From this letter we will see the very opposite. Philemon had given Paul joy by coming to Christ and Paul was going to ask Philemon for a favour in love.

Paul had never visited Colossae and the Lycus Valley where Philemon lived, but he did spend two years in Ephesus, and we are told that "all the

Jews and Greeks in the province of Asia heard the word of the Lord" (Acts 19:10). Maybe Philemon had visited Ephesus and heard Paul there; Colossae was in the province of Asia.

It would appear that Philemon was a wealthy man. He had a house with at least one guest room (Philemon 22), and the local church met there. He also owned slaves, one of whom was Onesimus. However, for some reason Onesimus had decided to run away. This was a serious thing for a slave to do, for if he was caught, he would be taken back to his master who could do with him as he wanted; imprison him, beat him, even have the slave put to death. Was Philemon a bad master? Had Onesimus been poorly or harshly treated? It is easy for us to say "No!" and point to the fact that Philemon was a Christian, but being a Christian doesn't always prevent people from behaving badly. However, from the glowing tones of what Paul wrote we gain the impression that Philemon treated his slaves in terms of Ephesians 6:9 and Colossians 4:1.

The picture is that Onesimus was a reluctant servant. Maybe he had just got fed up with being a slave! We do not know why the slave ran away, but we know that he did. We also know that he stole something (Philemon 18-19). He probably took some food and could have stolen money or some valuable items which he could sell for money. Having committed his crimes, Onesimus would then have put as much distance between him and Philemon as possible, but where would he go? Where do people go when they want to get lost? To the big city; to Rome, a thousand miles from Colossae! (1,600 km).

From Colossae he could have gone to Laodicea and then on to Ephesus. From there a boat across the Aegean Sea to Greece, maybe to Athens or Corinth. Continuing west he would come to the Adriatic and a boat to Italy, and on to Rome. (If the reader has a Bible atlas, it is interesting to look at the journey which Onesimus would have taken.) Or he could have travelled over-land from Colossae, going further and further north till he struck the Egnatian Way, where he would have gone west through Macedonia. Then he would have gone through such places as Philippi and Thessalonica, before coming to the Adriatic where, again, a boat would be needed to cross from Apollonia to Brundisium, on the heel of Italy. Then he would travel along the Appian Way to Rome.

How long would such a journey take Onesimus? We cannot tell. We do not know how much money he had. Did he take the shorter route and take two boats, or did he take the longer route which would require much more walking? Did he have to stop and work for food and money on the way? If he did so, would people find out that he was a runaway slave? I suspect he may have got out of Asia as quickly as possible, and I suspect he may have got to Rome, the big city, as soon as he possibly could. Once there, he could hide amongst the crowds. Philemon would never find him there. Onesimus would never be caught and taken back to Colossae. He was safe there, but….

Somehow or other Onesimus came into contact with Paul, and it was through Paul that Onesimus, like his master Philemon, came to believe in the

Lord Jesus Christ as his Saviour. Hence Paul could call Onesimus "my son" (twice in Philemon 10). Paul also referred to him as "our faithful and dear brother, who is one of you" (Colossians 4:9); a "dear" brother, yes, but a "faithful" one? Onesimus could not have been a believer long. Had his faith been tested?

We can only imagine the peace that came over Onesimus when he realised that Christ had died for his sins; that he was forgiven – even for running away and stealing from his master; that he was free – even though he was still a slave. However, that peace must have been shattered when Paul told him that the *Christian* thing to do was to return to Colossae and to face Philemon. I should imagine Onesimus' heart must have sunk, but it seems that this new-born babe in Christ was prepared to do the *Christian* thing, and this may have been why Paul called him "faithful" in Colossians 4:9.

And so this runaway slave, who was also a thief, was prepared to go back to see his master. Paul sent Tychicus with him, to keep him company

(Colossians 4:7-8). However, Onesimus was armed only with a letter from Paul, but having a common faith in Jesus Christ. Did that common faith and that letter secure Philemon's forgiveness? We do not know, but all of us hope that they did.

Philemon may be a short letter, but its historical background is rich, and having looked at it, we may well better understand the details of the letter.

Philemon:
Theologically

Philemon: Theologically

Verse 1: Paul, a prisoner of Christ Jesus, and Timothy our brother, To Philemon our dear friend and fellow worker.

As we have seen in our first section, Paul was a prisoner in Rome, under house arrest, waiting for his case to be heard by Caesar's court. By the time he wrote to Philemon, he had been under arrest for a number of years. He had been falsely accused by the Jewish leaders, poorly treated by the Roman governor Felix (who wanted a bribe) and by his replacement, Festus who, wanting to do the Jews a favour, was going to send Paul back to Jerusalem.

Then, after his appeal to Caesar, Paul was chained to a Roman soldier, and then came that harassing sea journey to Rome, with its shipwreck. Afterwards there was the waiting in Rome, the waiting and waiting for his case to be heard. How did Paul, a man of action, cope with all this? Did he get depressed? No! He considered himself neither a prisoner of the Jews, nor a prisoner of the Romans, but rather a prisoner of Christ Jesus. If he had been languishing in chains for years, then he considered that to be Christ's will. On previous occasions, during the period covered by the Acts of the Apostles, Paul had been miraculously freed from chains (Acts 16:22-38), and so had Peter (Acts 12:1-11). Thus if, during the Acts period, Paul was not freed by the Lord or an angel, then his only conclusion was that he was "a prisoner of Christ Jesus" and there must be some purpose in it.

As we mentioned earlier, when in Rome Paul was under house arrest and was free to receive visitors. One of these was Timothy, whom Paul called "our brother". This letter is addressed to Philemon, whom Paul calls "our dear friend and fellow-worker". As we have seen, Philemon was, indeed, a dear friend of Paul. He had come to know Jesus Christ through Paul's ministry. But he was also a "fellow-worker". He had opened his home to the

Christian church. Would he now open his heart to a Christian slave?

Verse 2: To Apphia our sister, to Archippus our fellow solider and to the church that meets in your home.

We know little about Apphia and Archippus. It is likely that these were members of Philemon's household. Apphia was possibly Philemon's wife Archippus his son. Apphia is mentioned nowhere else Scripture, but it was a common name in the area at that time. Archippus, however, is mentioned in Colossians 4: 17 where we read:

> Tell Archippus: "See to it that you complete the work you have received in the Lord."

We have no idea what work was being referring to, but obviously Archippus did. Paul called Archippus "our fellow soldier", a phrase also used of Epaphroditus in Philippians 2:25. This suggests that he was personally involved in the work of spreading the gospel or tending the church in his area. The inclusion of the church in the opening salutation suggests that Philemon's home was the regular meeting place of the church.

Verse 3: Grace to you and peace from God our Father and the Lord Jesus Christ.

In how many of Paul's letters does he open with "grace and peace"? It is an interesting exercise just to read the opening verses of each Paul's letters and to make a note of what he says about these wonderful words.

The Greek for "grace" is *charis,* while the Greek for "peace" is *eirene*, the Hebrew equivalent being *shalom.* The following is taken from page 9 of *Studies in Philippians* (published by the Open Bible Trust).

When Paul took and put together these two words "grace" and "peace", *charis* and *eirene,* he was doing something very wonderful. He was taking the everyday greeting phrases of two very distinct cultures. "Grace", *charis*, was the normal Greek greeting whilst "peace", , was the one with which the Hebrews greeted one another. Each of these words has a flavour of its own.

Charis is a lovely word. The basic idea is joy and pleasure or brightness and beauty, and is connected with the English word 'charm'. The other word, *eirene*, is a great comprehensive word which we translate 'peace', but he never means a negative peace – the absence of trouble and problems. It is a positive peace, corresponding to the total well-being of all individuals.

Everything for man's highest good comes from God, and it is certainly true of grace and peace. That peace which Christ gives us not the peace this world talks about. The true peace, we must seek "the peace of God, which transcends all understanding" (Philippians 4: 7).

Verse 4: I always thank my God as I remember you in my prayers.

Again, it is salutary to look through Paul's letters and see how many references there are prayer. (See *Unanswered Prayer* by Neville Stephens and

The Place of Prayer in an Age of Grace by Michael Penny, published by The Open Bible Trust). However, from this verse's point of view, we need to pay special attention to how many times Paul wrote such things as "I *always* thank my God as I remember you in my prayers".

He says "*always* thank" in 1 Corinthians 1:4; Colossians 1:3 and 1 Thessalonians 1:2. He says "*always* prayed" in Philippians 1:4. And has such phrases as "I have *not stopped* giving thanks for you, remembering you in my prayers" in Ephesians 1:16 and "I have *not stopped* praying for you" in Colossians 1:9.

When he wrote his later letters (such as Ephesians, Colossians, Philemon and Philippians) Paul was under house arrest in Rome and we can imagine that he had plenty of time to think about people and pray for them. However, even when he was free and busy (as when he wrote to the Corinthians and Thessalonians) he still found time to pray. And a frequent part of his prayers was to thank God for the people who had come to believe in the Lord Jesus Christ. Certainly he had some previous problems with the Corinthians. True, there were theological and practical problems with the Colossians. None-the-less Paul looked for the good in them and thanked God for them. We should do the same.

Verse 5: because I hear about your faith in the Lord Jesus and your love for all the saints.

Paul had probably heard the latest reports about Philemon's faith and love from Epaphras, when he reported to Paul on the Colossians (Colossians 1:7-8). The reason Paul gave for thanking God for Philemon was his "faith in the Lord Jesus" and his "love for all the saints". As the word for "faith", *pistis*, can also mean faithfulness, which may be the better meaning here as Paul goes on to talk about how Philemon had "refreshed the hearts of the saints" (v 7). Faith in Christ should always show itself in faithfulness to Christ's will and to His new commandment for Christians to love one another.

The "faith" and "love" are the same reasons given in such passages as Ephesians 1:15. However, if we consider the corrective teaching in Ephesians 4-6 we would say that their faith was suspect and their love deficient.

In doing that we would be comparing them with the goal of the Christian life, whereas Paul was comparing them with what they had been previously, at the start of the Christian life. Here is another lesson we can learn from Paul. It is certainly true that "all have sinned and come short of the glory of God" (Romans 3:23).

Thus we can find deficiencies in every believer … and that includes ourselves. We can point the finger at every believer … but we can also point a finger at the mirror. Rather than seeing how far people have to go in the Christian life, let us rather look and see how far they have come.

Epaphras reported to Paul both the strengths and weaknesses of the Colossian Christians. Paul praised them for the good, and wrote caring, corrective teaching.

Verse 6: I pray that you may be active in sharing your faith, so that you will have a full understanding of every good thing we have in Christ.

Why did Paul pray Philemon may be "active" in sharing his faith? Clearly Philemon had "love for all the saints" (v 5). He had also "refreshed the hearts of the saints" (v 7). So what was Paul wanting? It does not seem likely that Paul was referring to Philemon communicating his faith in Jesus Christ to others. Rather, this seems to be a prayer for Philemon to *do* something. This phrase would grab Philemon's attention, making him ask, "What is it Paul wants me to do?" It is an expression preparing Philemon for what was to come.

In many of Paul's prayers he uses the expression "so that" or just "that" or "in order that". These may tell us why Paul was praying for those things, or they may tell us what would be the consequences if that prayer was answered. Here, if Philemon was active in sharing his faith then he "will have full understanding of every good thing we have in Christ Jesus".

Some of the good things we have in Christ are forgiveness, love, peace, joy, happiness. We have these because we have accepted Christ's sacrifice for our sins. We now know that God loves us forgives us, and we need not fear Him when we stand before Him on the day of resurrection. Then we will be holy and blameless in His sight (Ephesians 1:3; 5:27; Colossians 1:22).

However, although as recipients we may have some appreciation of such things as love and forgiveness, we will never have a full understanding until we love and forgive those who have wronged us. This was what Paul was about to ask Philemon to do. If he could love and forgive Onesimus he would have a fuller understanding of Christ's love in forgiveness for him. And the same is true for us.

At this point Philemon may have been thinking that Paul had wanted him to do something, or give something from his material affluence. However, what Paul was about to ask would require Philemon to delve into the coffers of his heart and pull out an abundance of mercy, forgiveness, love and grace. Would Philemon be up to it?

Verse 7: Your love has given me great joy and encouragement, because you, brother, have refreshed the hearts of the saints.

We may not know what Philemon had done for his fellow-Christians in Corinth but, as mentioned earlier, Epaphras probably reported to Paul. Certainly he opened his home for the church to meet there. He had "refreshed the hearts of the saints". However, it seems he did much above and beyond the call of duty for Paul wrote "Your love has given me great joy". It also gave Paul "encouragement", encouragement for what he was about to ask Philemon to do. Had Philemon been magnanimous towards others?

Verse 8: Therefore, although in Christ I could be bold and order you to do what you ought to do ...

Paul, with respect to the world, was inferior to Philemon. Paul was impoverished in prison; Philemon was affluent and free. However, in earlier days Philemon had been saved under Paul's ministry and even though in prison and poor, Paul was still an apostle. As such Paul could have used his apostolic authority to order Philemon to do the right thing. However, that is not how one friend approaches the other. Also, Paul would want Philemon to accept Onesimus out of love and forgiveness, rather than out of duty or in obedience.

Verse 9: … yet I appeal to you on the basis of love. I then, as Paul – an old man and now also a prisoner of Christ Jesus - …

Although Paul could have appealed to Philemon as an apostle and an ambassador of Christ, he chose to appeal as an old man, and as a prisoner of Christ. Although Paul could have commanded Philemon, he chose to appeal in love. And as well as appealing to Philemon's love, he may well have been appealing to his sympathy, not sympathy for Onesimus, but sympathy for Paul who was an old man in prison and who was about to make a request for a young man, and young convert to Christ.

Verse 10: I appeal to you for my son Onesimus, who became my son while I was in chains.

Was Onesimus present, or had Tychicus told him to wait somewhere while he delivered a letter? If so, then on reading these words, this would have been the first Philemon had heard about Onesimus.

First there was the appeal, but Paul did not say what he wanted, and then came the news that Onesimus was now Christian. And amazingly, both Philemon and Onesimus were brought to Christ by the same person, Paul. Two very different people, into very different places, into very different circumstances, yet Paul had reached them both. What was it Paul wrote in 1 Corinthians 9:22? "To the weak I became weak, to win the weak. I have become all things to all men so that by all possible means I might save some."

Would this news of Onesimus becoming a Christian through Paul have warmed Philemon's heart?

Verse 11: Formerly he was useless to you, but now he has become useful both to you and to me.

The name 'Onesimus' means 'useful' or 'profitable'. Here Paul makes a double play on his name. He uses both an antonym, "useless" and a synonym "useful". Formerly Onesimus did not live up to his name; "he was useless to you". However, having become a Christian, he now does live up to that name; "he has become useful both to you and to me".

Onesimus had become useful to Paul, no doubt rendering many services to the man who was under house arrest in Rome. Perhaps at this point Philemon stopped reading and asked Tychicus what Onesimus had done for Paul. However, Paul also wrote that already Onesimus had become useful to Philemon, but what, at this point, had the slave done for his master? By the very act returning of his own free will Onesimus showed Philemon how useful he had become, and would be in the future. For a new, young Christian slave, to be willing to return 1,000 miles (1,600 km.) to his former master, not knowing what reception he would receive, is staggering. Onesimus is one of the unsung heroes of the Bible. The Christian conviction to do the right thing, in one so young in the faith, is an example to us all.

Verse 12: I am sending him – who is my very heart – back to you.

Having referred to Onesimus as "my son", Paul then used a very strong, emotional phrase, saying that Onesimus "is my very heart". This emphasises the deep affection Paul had for this slave.

Verse 13: I would have liked to keep him with me so that he could take your place in helping me while I am in chains for the gospel.

Clearly to keep Onesimus with him in Rome, but he could not do so. First of all, if he had done so, he would have been breaking the law. However, to have kept Onesimus without Philemon's agreement would have been a breach of his friendship in fellowship with Philemon.

As we have said, Paul was under house arrest in Rome, chained to a Roman guard, but free to receive whoever chose to come and visit him. At times he had such prominent people as Timothy, but he could be sent off on long journeys to such places as Philippi (Philippians 2:19).

The physician, Luke, was there for his health needs. However, who would do those day to day tasks, the looking after of Paul and his guests? Was that Onesimus' role? Or could Onesimus write? Was that his job as a slave for Philemon?

Paul could certainly have used a writer, and some have suggested that the letter to the Colossians, while dictated by Paul, was penned by Tychicus and Onesimus. And some have suggested that this letter to Philemon was penned by Onesimus. If so, we can only imagine the surprise there must have been on Philemon's face when he opened the letter from Paul to see it written in the familiar script of his slave.

What did Paul mean by I "would have liked to keep him with me so that *he could take your place in helping me while I am in chains for the gospel*"? As we have mentioned, it was Epaphras who had taken news of the Colossians, including Philemon, to Paul in Rome. Possibly Epaphras had gone to see Philemon before he left, asking if Philemon had any message for Paul. Possibly Philemon may have said words to the effect that he wished he could go to Rome so that he could serve and wait on Paul there. Obviously he was unable to do so, his runaway slave had done just that.

Verse 14: But I did not want to do anything without your consent, so that any favour you do will be spontaneous and not forced.

Clearly Paul wanted Philemon to send Onesimus back to Rome to minister to his needs. However, there is no command, and even the appeal is dropped. Now this is just a favour asked, from one friend to another. Did Philemon agree to his slave returning to Rome? There is no mention of it, nor even of Onesimus, in Paul's letters written after this time –Philippians, Titus and 1 & 2 Timothy.

Verse 15: Perhaps the reason he was separated from you a little while was that you might have him back for good...

Obviously, Paul did not want to pressurise Philemon into returning his slave to Rome. Such an act must be spontaneous. Thus Paul backs off, stating that the short separation could result in Philemon having Onesimus "back for good".

Here Paul almost implies that there was a purpose in this separation; that it was, in some way or other, an act of God. This is unlikely as Onesimus had probably broken the law at least twice, in running away and in stealing.

What is more likely is that the Lord over-ruled this sorry state of affairs. As Paul put it, "And we know that in all things God works for the good of those who love him, who have been called according to his purpose" (Romans 8:28). God is able to turn even sin to the good, as we see with the Joseph's brothers selling him into slavery in Egypt.

Onesimus served as a slave in a Christian household. He worked for a Christian man who had great faith in Christ and who had much love for all the saints, who had refreshed the hearts of the saints. None-the-less Philemon's Christianity had not penetrated Onesimus' heart. This separation had resulted in Onesimus coming to believe in Christ. In this way it was a benefit for Onesimus. However, due to his help, the separation was also a benefit to Paul, and now it could be to the benefit of Philemon, as Onesimus would be back for good, as now he was a fellow-Christian.

As a slave Onesimus could be separated from Philemon in a number of ways; by being sold, by being set free, by being redeemed by a benefactor and, of course, by prison or death. However, as fellow-Christians they were bound together in Christ for eternity.

Verse 16: ... no longer as a slave, but better than a slave, as a dear brother. He is very dear to me but even dearer to you, both as a man and as a brother in the Lord.

As Philemon read this later, possibly pausing to ask Tychicus the details, one can imagine that he was slowly coming to terms with expecting back this runaway slave ... as a slave. Maybe his generosity could extend to him returning Onesimus to Rome and Paul. However, Paul's request now takes a different turn.

No longer was he asking Philemon to accept a runaway slave, a Christian runaway slave, Philemon was now being asked to accept him back not just as a slave, but "as a dear brother". What did Philemon think of that? If he accepted a disobedient slave back as a brother, what about some of his other faithful slaves who were Christians? How should he treat them?

Was Paul, here, in effect, asking Philemon to give Onesimus his freedom? If he was, what would be the consequences in Philemon's household?

Should he set all the slaves free? Should he not use slaves? Who would do the work? If he made Onesimus a freedman, would he stay on? Would the other slaves stay on as workers if they were freed? These, and many other questions, must have run through Philemon's head. How did he respond? We do not know!

Verse 17: So if you consider me a partner, welcome him as you would welcome me.

And now comes the final request, and Paul uses the word "partner", implying that Philemon was effectively and importantly involved in some aspect of the ministry, maybe more than just the church meeting in his home. "So… if you consider me a partner," wrote Paul, "welcome him as you would welcome me." Welcome this slave as a free man! Welcome this slave is a free Christian brother! Welcome this slave as the Apostle Paul! Paul's meaning must now have been abundantly obvious to Philemon. If you consider yourself a partner with Paul, a fellow-worker (v 1), then except this slave back, forgive him, set him free, and return him to Rome. Could Philemon do it? Did he do it?

Verse 18: If he has done you any wrong or owes you anything, charge it to me.

However, if Philemon wished to reclaim from Onesimus the value of what he had stolen, or payment for the work missed while absent, then Paul was prepared to pay it. He did not want his friend being out of pocket. Maybe Paul was willing to pay Philemon for the time Onesimus had been away, spent serving Paul in Rome. And Paul emphasises this in the next verse.

Verse 19: I, Paul, am writing this with my own hand. I will pay it back – not to mention that you owe me your very self.

Back in Rome, having dictated the letter, Paul then grabbed the pen and wrote this note with his own hand, as best he could with chains on his wrists. He wrote that he would repay whatever was owed by Onesimus. He would be Onesimus' guarantor, but from where would Paul get the money? As he was under house arrest, Paul would have to pay for the rent of the house, the wages of the soldier, and would have to provide food for both himself and the soldier. This could be quite expensive and Paul was dependent on the gifts of others. However, various individuals and groups sent money (e.g. Philippians 4:10-19). Paul was willing to divert such gifts away from his needs to Philemon to make reparations for the wrong-doing of Onesimus. But will the wealthy, free man want such a gift from the poor, imprisoned Paul? It is doubtful. After all, he owed his faith in Christ, and all the spiritual blessings that ensued, from Paul's ministry.

Verse 20: I do wish, brother, that I may have some benefit from you in the Lord; refresh my heart in Christ.

Paul makes it clear that he would like Onesimus returned to him but wishing that he may have some "benefit". This word "benefit" uses the verb from which the name 'Onesimus' is derived. To see Onesimus back in Rome would refresh Paul's heart.

Verse 21: Confident of your obedience, I write to you, knowing that you will do even more than I ask.

Although Paul dictated verses 1-18, at verse 19 he took up the pen and it seems likely that he kept it, writing the rest of the letter. This verse says, "I write to you".

Paul was confident of Philemon's obedience, not his orders, but to his appeal, to his request for a favour. Paul was more than confident. He stated than Philemon would do even more than he asked. Would Philemon overlook stolen money or property? Would he not ask Paul for repayment?

Verse 22: And one thing more: Prepare a guest room for me, because I hope to be restored to you in answer to your prayers.

Paul was confident that his case before Caesar's court would go well. It was just a matter of waiting. Some months later, when he wrote to the Philippians, he was confident that he would be released soon (Philippians 2:24), and said that he intended to visit them. It seems that Paul was released and from his last letters –Titus and 1 & 2 Timothy, we know that he visited such places as Macedonia and Ephesus (1 Timothy 1:13); Crete and Nicopolis (Titus 1: 15; 3:12); Corinth, Miletus and Troas (2 Timothy 4: 13, 20), before being re-arrested and taken back to Rome (2 Timothy 1:17). There is, however, no mention of him getting to Colossae, Ephesus being the nearest place.

Verse 23: Epaphras, my fellow prisoner in Christ Jesus, sends you greetings.

Epaphras was the one who had taken the gospel to Colossae and the Lycus Valley (Colossians 1:7-8) and so he was known by Philemon and his household. Thus it is appropriate that he should be mentioned first. However, why he was called a "fellow-prisoner" we do not know. It appears that he had gone up from Colossae to Rome to report to Paul some of the problems with the Colossian church. Weather at some other time he and Paul had been imprisoned, we do not know.

Verse 24: And so do Mark, Aristarchus, Demas and Luke, my fellow workers.

This list of people is the same as at the end of Colossians (4: 1-14), with the exception of Jesus-Justus who may have been away at the time Paul wrote to Philemon. They are all called "fellow–workers".

Verse 25: The grace of the Lord Jesus Christ be with your spirit.

In how many of Paul's letters does he close with "grace"? It is an interesting exercise just to read the closing verses of each of Paul's letters, to see how useful this wonderful word is.

Philemon:
Practically

Philemon: Practically

In 2 Timothy 3:16 – 17 we read:

> All Scripture is God-breathed and is useful for teaching, rebuking, correcting and training in righteousness, so that the man of God maybe thoroughly equipped for every good work.

If this is the case, what can we find useful in this letter to Philemon? It may be a salutary exercise to re-read the letter, thinking what may or may not apply to us. A letter to a slave master, written almost 2,000 years ago, may seem totally inappropriate to a free industrialised society. However, if we think that, we would be wrong.

There are many lessons in this letter which are applicable to us today. The following strike a chord with me.

Lesson 1:

When commenting on verse 4 we noted that Paul had some serious problems with the Corinthians and the Colossians and, indeed, with most of the churches and Christian groups of his time. None-the-less, Paul looked for the good in them and thanked God for them. We should do the same.

Lesson 2:

When commenting on verse 5, we observed that if we consider the corrective teaching in such passages as Ephesians 4-6 or Colossians 3-4, we would challenge the faith and question the love of these people. Did they really believe this? However, if we did that we would be comparing them with the best, with Christ, with the maturity expected from long established Christians. By contrast, it seems, Paul compared them with what they had been previously, maybe with what they were even before they were Christians. Here is another lesson we can learn from Paul.

None of us is righteous (Romans 3:10) and it is most certainly true that "all have sinned and come short of the glory of God" (Romans 3:23). Thus if we want, we can find deficiencies in every believer, including ourselves. We can point the finger at every believer, but we should also point the finger at ourselves. Rather than seeing how far people have to go, let us rather look back and see how far they have come.

Lesson 3:

In verse 6 we read that if Philemon was active in sharing his faith then he would have full understanding of every good thing we have in Christ Jesus. As we mentioned, these good things include love and forgiveness, as well as joy and peace. We have these because we believe Christ died for our sins. We know that God loves us and forgives us, and we need never fear Him. However, although we may have some appreciation of such things as love and forgiveness, as recipients, we will never have a full understanding of them until we love and forgive those who have wronged us.

Lesson 4:

When we first become believers there are a number of sins that we easily throw away, but there are some which take longer to get under control. However, these sins of "commission" (doing the wrong things) can sometimes be far easier to deal with than the sins of "omission" (not doing the right things). In this letter we read of a new, young, Christian convert, a slave, who was willing to return 1,000 miles (1,600 km.) to his former master, not knowing what reception he would receive. Would he be imprisoned, beaten, or sold in the slave market to who know whom?

It would have been so easy for Onesimus to have opted out, not go, and to give up his Christianity, but no! He went, and to me Onesimus is one of the unsung heroes of the Bible. The Christian conviction to do the right thing in one so young in the faith is an example to each and every one of us.

Lesson 5:

The fifth lesson I include here is a quotation from *Mediations on Paul's Post–Acts Ministry* by R. B. Shiflet and Michael Penny (OBT).

> In a letter, Paul makes the appeal to Philemon concerning this slave: "so if you consider me a partner, welcome him as you would welcome me. If he has done you any wrong or owes you anything, charge it to me. I, Paul, am writing this with my own hand. I will pay it back – not to mention that you owe me your very self" (vs 17-19).
>
> This is such a precious picture of the work of our Lord Jesus on our behalf. We, in the past, were spiritually dead, but thanks to the grace of God, we receive from Him the very righteousness of Christ Who can say to the Father, "If he has wronged you, or owes you ought, put to My account; I paid it at Calvary; whatever love You have for Me, put it on his account."
>
> How we should rejoice in the work of our Lord that is portrayed here in Philemon!

Would we, as Christians, be prepared to pay for the wrongs of a fellow-Christian? This takes *Lesson 3* to a much deeper level.

Lesson 6:

This final lesson comes from a personal letter written to me by Roger Barnett. He noticed several parallels between Onesimus and ourselves.

Onesimus	*Christians*
His master *chose* him.	Our Master *chose* us.
His master paid a *price* for him.	He paid a dreadful *price* for us.
This was before Onesimus was found to be *useless*.	This was while we were yet sinners and *useless* to Him.
He was *useless* because he would *not* obey and accept the authority of his	We were sinners, *disobeying* our Master.

master: a picture of sin.	
He sinned further by *running away.*	We went *astray*, every one to his own way.
The *gospel* was *preached* to him.	We *heard* the *gospel* of Christ Jesus.
He was *converted* – in Christ Jesus.	We repented and were *converted.*
His master, Philemon, *accepted* his repentance and received him because he was *in Christ.*	We are *accepted in Christ.*
He became a *useful servant* to his master, *obeying his word.*	We are now enabled to be *useful servants* for Him, *obeying His Word.*

Also in this series

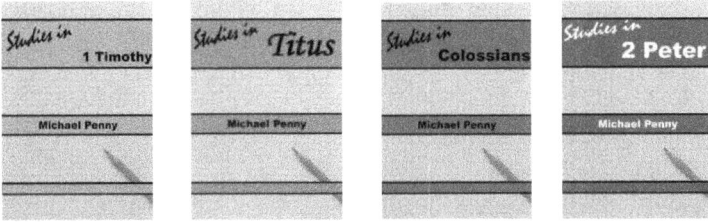

Michael Penny has written, or edited, a number of other books in this series including:

- **Studies in 1 Thessalonians**
- **Studies in 2 Thessalonians**
- **Studies in Colossians**
- **Studies in Philemon**
- **Studies in Philippians**
- **Studies in 1 Timothy**
- **Studies in 2 Timothy**
- **Studies in Titus**
- **Studies in 2 Peter**
- **Studies in John's Epistles**
- **Studies in Jude**
- **Studies in Ruth**

These are also available as eBooks and KDP paperbacks.
Details from www.obt.org.uk

About the author

Michael Penny was born in Ebbw Vale, Gwent, Wales in 1943. He read Mathematics at the University of Reading, before teaching for twelve years and becoming the Director of Mathematics and Business Studies at Queen Mary's College Basingstoke in Hampshire, England. In 1978 he entered Christian publishing, and in 1984 became the administrator of The Open Bible Trust.

He held this position for seven years, before moving to the USA and becoming pastor of Grace Church in New Berlin, Wisconsin. He returned to Britain in 1999, and is at present the Administrator and Editor of The Open Bible Trust. From 2010 he has been Chairman of Churches Together in Reading, where he speaks in a number of churches of different denominations. He is also a member of the Advisory Committee to Reading University Christian Union and a chaplain at Reading College.

He is lead chaplain for Activate Learning and has set up chaplaincy teams in a number of their colleges including Reading College, The City of Oxford College, Bracknell and Wokingham College, and Blackbird Leys College.

He lives near Reading with his wife and has appeared on Premier Radio and BBC Radio Berkshire many times. He has made several speaking tours of America, Canada, Australia, New Zealand and the Netherlands, as well as others to South Africa and the Philippines. Some of his writings have been translated into German and Russian.

Also by Michael Penny

He has written many books including:

40 Problem Passages,
Galatians: Interpretation and Application,
Joel's Prophecy: Past and Future,
Approaching the Bible,
The Miracles of the Apostles,
The Manual on the Gospel of John
The Bible! Myth or Message?

His latest three books are:

James: His life and letter
Peter: His life and letters.
Paul: A Missionary of Genius

He has also written three with W M Henry:

The Will of God: Past and Present
Following Philippians
Abraham and his seed (with chapters by Sylvia Penny also)

Further details of the books on these pages, and the next, can be seen on

www.obt.org.uk

The books are available from that website and from

The Open Bible Trust
Fordland Mount, Upper Basildon,
Reading, RG8 8LU, UK.

They are also available as
eBooks from Amazon and Apple,
and as KDP paperbacks from Amazon

Further reading

The Miracles of the Apostles
Michael Penny

Why did the Apostles perform miracles?
Why were they able to perform them?
What was the purpose of the miracles?
What did they signify to the Jews?
Why did the Gentiles misunderstand them?
Why was Paul, later, not able to heal?
When did the miracles cease?
Why did they cease?

This book answers these questions, explains the significance and purpose of each type of miracle performed by the Apostles, and makes it clear why such miracles are not in evidence today.

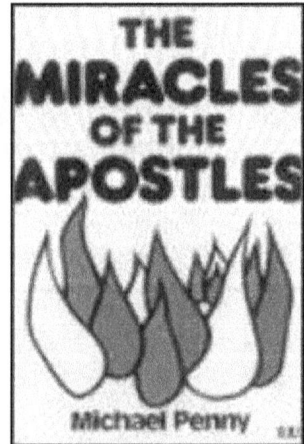

THE MIRACLES OF THE APOSTLES

Michael Penny

Salvation

Safe and Secure

Sylvia Penny

This important book is a
thorough treatment of the
subject of salvation, asking such
questions as …

- What is it, exactly, that saves us?
- Is salvation secure?
- Can it be lost?
- What is 'conditional security'?

It deals with a wide number of issues such as …

- Salvation and works
- The doctrine of rewards
- Lordship salvation
- Free grace theology
- Assurance of salvation
- Why people lose their faith

Search magazine

Michael Penny is editor of *Search* magazine.

About this book

Studies in Philemon
Historically; Theologically; Practically

Paul's little letter to his friend Philemon, concerning Philemon's runaway slave Onesimus, may, at first glance, have little to do with modern man in the twenty-first century. However, nothing could be further from the truth.

- This publication first sets the scene historically, enabling the reader to more fully understand the background which caused Paul to write this letter.
- Next the author gives a theological exposition of these twenty five verses, ensuring the reader understands what Paul has written.
- Lastly, this letter is reviewed with present-day applications in mind and six important lessons are drawn from its pages, lessons

from which all Christians can benefit and learn.